Encounter *with* Mercy

A STEP-BY STEP GUIDE TO THE SACRAMENT OF RECONCILIATION

Nihil Obstat
Imprimatur
✠ Most Reverend Henry J. Mansell
Archbishop of Hartford
December 9, 2009

ISBN 978-1-933271-36-1

Printed in the United States of America

TABLE OF CONTENTS

FOREWORD

The sacrament of Penance or Reconciliation is one of the greatest gifts which the Lord Jesus gave to his Church. It is intimately related to and makes present in each generation the saving grace of the death and resurrection of Jesus. Christ willed that this wonderful sacrament would be the ordinary means through which members of the Church would receive the forgiveness of sins and the strength to live the Christian life. Through the ministry of priests, Christ forgives our sins and continues to build up his Body, the Church.

Encounter with Mercy endeavors to make this gift of Christ to his Church more widely understood and accepted in the lives of Catholics. The clear and straightforward explanation of the sacrament, along with stories of those who have returned to confession after a lengthy absence, motivates us to have a greater appreciation for this sacrament and to make ever greater use of it. The explanations regarding the examining of our consciences and the actual celebration of the sacrament are of practical help to anyone who wishes to go to confession with greater devotion, or to anyone who is returning to confession after a lengthy absence.

I am confident that this book will be a help in renewing the practice of regular confession, so much desired by Pope John Paul II and Pope Benedict XVI.

Justin Cardinal Rigali
January 5, 2010

INTRODUCTION: The Crisis of Love

Pope Benedict XVI said it best: "How can one not recognize in our age … confession must be rediscovered and proposed anew?"[1] In his homily during Holy Mass at Nationals Park in Washington, D.C., on April 17, 2008, the Pope said, "Through the surpassing power of Christ's grace, entrusted to frail human ministers, the Church is constantly reborn and each of us is given the hope of a new beginning. …To a great extent, the renewal of the Church in America and throughout the world depends on the renewal of the practice of Penance and the growth in holiness which that sacrament both inspires and accomplishes."

When he speaks about confession, Pope Benedict speaks with the longing of a father. "How many people in difficulty seek the comfort and consolation of Christ! How many penitents find in confession the peace and joy that they sought for so long!"

He's the second pope of the 21st century to emphasize confession. Pope John Paul II was its first crusader.

In his 2001 signature document titled "At the Beginning of the New Millennium" (the apostolic letter *Novo Millennio Ineunte),* he made promoting the sacrament of reconciliation one of the two top priorities for the Church in our time. (The other one was Sunday Mass.)

He asked bishops in particular to have "courage, confidence and creativity" in reestablishing the sacrament of confession in their diocese.

When John Paul talked about crisis in the Church, he often singled out the crisis of confession. In his 2002 Holy Thursday letter to priests, the Pope noted a disturbing drop in attendance at confession and reiterated three times that people in a state of serious sin should not receive Communion without going to confession first.

He pleaded: "My dear brothers in the priesthood ... I feel a pressing need to urge you, as I did last year, to rediscover for yourselves and to help others to rediscover the beauty of the sacrament of reconciliation.

"In recent decades and for a variety of reasons the sacrament has passed through a crisis. More than once I have drawn attention to this fact, even making it the theme of a gathering of the synod of bishops."

He said that, because of the confession crisis, there was a crisis in the belief in sin, and that this had led directly to specific scandals in the Church.

Then, on the feast of Divine Mercy in 2002, John Paul put his plea for more confession and proper confession into an apostolic letter all its own, giving it an especially pointed *motu proprio* status.

To follow that up, he wrote an encyclical about the Eucharist *(Ecclesia de Eucharistia)* that stressed confession. For those accustomed to Church documents, the language Pope John Paul II used at one point is extraordinary – it is a kind of formal declaration:

"I therefore desire to reaffirm that in the Church there remains in force, now and in the future, the rule by which the Council of Trent gave concrete expression to the Apostle Paul's stern warning when it affirmed that, in order to receive the Eucharist in a worthy manner, 'one must first confess one's sins, when one is aware of mortal sin.'"

He declared a year of the Eucharist for 2004-2005. Halfway through it, he died, and Pope Benedict XVI became pope.

"My Pontificate begins in a particularly meaningful way as the Church is living the special year dedicated to the Eucharist," said the new Holy Father in his first message. "How could I fail to see this providential coincidence?"

Benedict presided over a synod on the Eucharist in Rome, and he summed up its findings in his own document, "The Sacrament of Love" (The post-synodal apostolic exhortation *Sacramentum caritatis).*

He emphasized "the intrinsic connection between the Eucharist and the sacrament of reconciliation" and taught that "all priests should dedicate themselves with generosity, commitment, and competency to administering the sacrament of reconciliation."

It's a message he has made his own in less formal settings.

"Dear brothers," he told priests at the Vatican, "let us follow the example of the saints, in particular those who were almost exclusively dedicated to the ministry of the confessional. Among them are St. Jean-Marie Vianney, St. Leopold Mandic, and closer to us, St. Pio of Pietrelcina. ... May the priest not forget that in this sacrament he is called to take on the role of father, spiritual guide, teacher, and educator" *(Address to the Confessors Who Serve in the Four Papal Basilicas in Rome,* February 19, 2007).

Thus the story of the Church in the 21st century – the century we have been entrusted with beginning – is the story of our Holy Fathers in Rome alternately challenging us, pleading with us, and urging us to rediscover confession.

They understand that the confessional is a unique place where we are purified in the fire of Christ's love, and the crisis of the confessional isn't merely a crisis about an old ritual passing away or a helpful practice being neglected.

It was – and is – a crisis of love. ✣

[1]*Taken from Pope Benedict XVI's address to the confessors who serve in the four major basilicas of Rome, February 19, 2007.*

7 SEEKERS' STORIES

You don't have to just take the popes' word for it. Ask the many people who have discovered confession as a source of great peace in their lives – usually on a Saturday afternoon.

1. THE GRATEFUL PENITENT

Many of us may have seen a similar scenario to this one that played out in a Connecticut church on a Saturday afternoon recently.

A nicely dressed man who looked anxious and upset walked into a church, squinted at the confessional, and couldn't tell if there was a priest in it or not. Turning to another person in the church he pointed at the confessional curtain and whispered loudly, "Is there a priest in there?"

He didn't care what priest – he needed a priest. Any priest.

"Yes," came the answer.

He barely acknowledged the help, and hurriedly entered the confessional.

After a few minutes he emerged again, looking like a different person. Gone was the haunted expression on his face. Gone was the urgency and anxiety. He was a man set free.

He smiled at the person who had merely pointed out the obvious. Then he silently mouthed the words "Thank you" with the gratitude of someone who had just been handed an antidote to rattlesnake poison!

2. THE ULTIMATE THERAPY

Here's a story that happened recently in California. This story is rarer than the first, but it's not as rare as you might think.

A teenage girl's whole character suddenly seemed to change one week. Her parents could even name the day she changed. She became moody, preoccupied, a shell of her carefree, kind, and cheerful self. After seeing her in a funk for weeks, they finally figured there must be something seriously wrong. They took her to counseling.

Counselors are often able to do wonders for people who suffer from clinical depression and anxiety. Theirs is a noble healing profession. But, in this case, the parents were sad to see that the therapy didn't help. Their daughter had seasons of improvement, but always ended up back in a distracted, unhappy state. This continued throughout her college years, and she still suffered when she began a teaching career after college.

It was a coincidence that one of her therapists met her outside one Saturday afternoon, and it was a coincidence that it was raining. The two stepped out of the rain into the nearest building: a Catholic church. As they sat and talked, the girl saw people lining up for confession. One by one they entered the confessional, then emerged. She remembered that she had gone to confession as a child. And she suddenly urgently felt like it was an important answer to the problem she had suffered ever since that day long ago.

She asked the therapist if she thought it was a good idea for her to go confession. This particular therapist said, "No, it's not a good idea." Confession might just make her feel guilty. But against her therapist's advice, and before she could stop her, she ducked into the confessional.

She emerged smiling, the first smile the therapist had ever seen on her young patient. The therapist noted that, in the days, weeks, and months that followed, the girl was no longer troubled with her old moodiness and unhappiness.

The therapist started to look into confession more, and then she herself decided to enter the Church. Now she counsels regular confession for all her Catholic patients.

3. THE TRIUMPHANT RETURN

Here's another true story. This one is about a woman in Ohio. She had been away from confession for fourteen years when she somehow felt God calling her back to the faith of her childhood.

"When I walked into the church I grew up in," she says, "God spoke to me loud and clear. He said, 'Welcome home, my child. I have been waiting for you to come back!'"

She started attending Sunday Mass. But it was not enough to satisfy her. "I really wanted to receive the Eucharist," she says. "I knew that in order to do that, I would have to confess all the mortal sins I had committed in the last fourteen years."

As she prepared to make her confession, Tina was confident in God's mercy. "It was like the Holy Spirit was giving me the courage to go through with this," she recalls.

When Saturday finally arrived, she went to church in the afternoon, ready to make a sincere confession and eager to receive forgiveness. In her nervousness and excitement, she mistakenly opened the wrong door and found herself face-to-face with the startled priest.

Despite the awkward start, she figured out what to do and made her confession. Afterward, she felt nothing but joy. "I felt light as a feather," she says. "My sins were forgiven, and I could receive Communion the next day. It was one of the most joyful days I can remember."

4. A CHILD SHALL LEAD THEM

Many of us can relate to one man's return to confession at the prompting of his son. He's a Michigan dad. Bob's son was preparing for his first Communion, and he asked his dad if he would be going to confession, too.

"My heart started to pound," says the dad. "After all, it had been twenty-five years since I had entered a confessional."

He would feel like a hypocrite, though, if he didn't go. And he figured he had to be a good example to his son. So he and his wife both went to confession for the first time in decades.

"It was a pivotal moment in our fully embracing the beautiful gift of our Catholic faith, a moment of conversion for both of us," he says.

His wife adds, "Isn't it so like Christ to come to us through our children?"

5. MERCY IS FOR ALL

Faith & Family magazine did a story called "After Abortion, Hope for Healing." The writer spoke to women who were battling feelings of despair after having an abortion. It was surprising how often these women mentioned confession as a key to their healing.

Theresa Bonapartis, cofounder of a post-abortion ministry, told her story. "I shut down emotionally and just let the abortion happen to me. After that, my life took a downward plunge. Thoughts of death were a consolation. I hated myself."

It was years later that she began to find strength through reading the Bible and praying. "I began to attend Mass, but I was uncomfortable. I was sure that everyone knew. I made spiritual progress, but I was severely depressed. Every day it was a challenge to get out of bed and care for my boys.

"Then, something a priest said offered me hope. I was attending a parents' meeting for my older son's first penance and first holy Communion. The priest talked about the mercy of God. He told us that God forgives all sin. 'God even forgives the sin of abortion,' he said.

"I couldn't believe my ears. I thought my sin was unforgivable. Confession was my road to healing."

She describes her restoration this way: "I climbed on the Cross with Christ, and instead of the suffering we see when we gaze upon him crucified, I saw in him the only love capable of taking away my pain."

6. BURNING THE LIST

All of us have more sins than we might admit to ourselves. A twenty-one-year-old man tells the story of how he entered the Church and, to make his first confession, underwent a thorough examination of conscience, writing down his sins. He was startled by the list of sins he compiled.

"It was impossible to have such a list and not be contrite," he says. "I was very eager to confess."

He was also nervous. "I was scared that my ignorance would be embarrassing," he says. Despite his jitters, the confession went smoothly. After giving him absolution, the priest suggested that he might want to burn the list of sins he had written out.

"I did," says the young man, "with the same light heart I've grown familiar with on Saturday afternoons since."

7. REDISCOVERING WHAT YOU KNOW

Even those who already go can rediscover confession. A Maryland woman was no stranger to the confessional when she rediscovered its power.

Several years ago, after making a retreat for the first time, she was determined to make a general confession. The equivalent of a physical for the soul, a general confession is not strictly necessary, but it is helpful for finding and putting to rest problems you may have been avoiding. In it, you confess all the sins of your life – or those since your last general confession.

"I was very nervous about this," says the woman. "I was not the least bit proud of my past life and had dodged many an opportunity for a general confession." Preferring anonymity, she went to a priest at a church she doesn't normally attend.

"I screwed up my courage and went," she says. "I don't know what I expected, but I was relieved when the priest said, 'Wow! That must have taken a lot of courage!'"

She remembers the feeling of complete and total relief that followed. "As I reflect on my life, that occasion of grace stands out as remarkable," she says. "By God's grace, from that point forth I was truly converted and turned to walk with Christ." ✣

10 REASONS TO GO TO CONFESSION

Those seven seekers discovered that confession is simple but its results can astonish. Just like the basic Christian story. In the fullness of time, God became man to save us from our sins. And in our own time, God still comes to us through his ministers to save us from our sins.

Jesus was both man and God. The sacraments, too, are both material and divine channels. The sacraments have both human and spiritual dimensions to them. Let's look at both.

5 Human Reasons to Confess

1. SIN AGGRAVATES YOU.

The Catechism says, "Sin is an offense against reason, truth, and right conscience; it is failure in genuine love for God and neighbor ... it has been defined as 'an utterance, a deed, or a desire contrary to the eternal law'" (CCC, 1849). Sin leads to depression and anxiety. Psychologists recognize this phenomenon. The wrong we've done haunts us. We can't ignore it. That's because to sin isn't just to break an arbitrary rule. It's to commit a violation of the plan for happy living, one that's built into our very being. We live in a world made by God and, whether we like it or not, his rules must be respected. The only way to achieve harmony is to rid ourselves of sin.

2. SIN MAKES YOU AGGRAVATING.

The ancient philosopher Aristotle said that we are defined by our choices. He was right. Our good choices make us better. Our bad choices make us worse. Our sins become part of who we are and shape our personality, bending us one way or another – unless we fix them.

3. WE NEED TO SAY IT.

Human beings are hardwired to be verbal and communicative. For us, it's not enough to be sorry. We need to name our deed and express our sorrow in speech. If you break something that's important to a friend, you will want to say, "I'm sorry," and you will want to do whatever you can to fix or replace what you broke. You wouldn't feel satisfied with a general feeling of remorse.

4. CONFESSING HELPS YOU KNOW YOURSELF.

Our egos have a way of playing tricks on us. Sometimes we nurture a false sense of security about the things we need to change. We convince ourselves that we are righteous and good. Other times, we obsess about faults and blow them out of proportion. Confession forces us to look at our lives objectively – and gives us a second opinion (the priest's).

5. CONFESSING STRENGTHENS US.

Who's stronger – the one who hides from her past or the one who confronts it? The one who studiously ignores his sins, or the one who confronts them, deals with them, and moves on? As the Catechism puts it, "Sin creates a proclivity to sin" (CCC, 1865). Get rid of it and you'll find you are more able to avoid the sin in the future.

5 Spiritual Reasons to Confess

1. FREEDOM MEANS THAT CHOICES COUNT.

We too easily accept the world's common understanding of freedom: We can do whatever suits our preferences as long as our choices don't hurt anyone else. But true freedom is the freedom to do what's right, not what the law says we have a right to do. Stated another way, true freedom means our choices count. As the Catechism points out, unconfessed mortal sin "causes exclusion from Christ's kingdom and the eternal death of hell, for our freedom has the power to make choices for ever, with no turning back" (CCC, 1861).

2. CONFESSION MAKES YOU FREER.

As people leave the confessional, they smile the smile of people who have had a heavy burden lifted from their shoulders. They no longer need to worry about the past. They can now make new choices – choices *for* God's way, not against it.

As Pope Benedict XVI put it during a meeting with children in St. Peter's Square on October 15, 2005: "This cleansing of the soul which Jesus gives us in the sacrament of confession helps us to make our consciences more alert, more open, and hence, it also helps us to mature spiritually and as human persons."

3. CONFESSION IS A PERSONAL ENCOUNTER WITH CHRIST.

What does this mean? Look at a Christmas crèche: The shepherds' awe, the magi's humility. Look at the crucifixion: the gratitude, repentance, joy and peace. Meeting Christ in the confessional can give us all of that.

4. CONFESSING MORTAL SIN IS REQUIRED.

You can't go to Communion – or be at peace with God – without confessing mortal sins. This is bare-minimum Christianity, one of the precepts of the Church. You must confess sins once a year, and as soon as possible when you are aware of committing a mortal sin.

As Pope Benedict XVI put it, confession is "necessary when you have committed a really serious sin, when you have deeply offended Jesus so that your friendship is destroyed and you have to start again. Only in that case, when you are in a state of 'mortal' sin, in other words, grave sin, is it necessary to go to confession before Communion" (Pope Benedict's meeting with children, St. Peter's Square, October 15, 2005).

Confession Definition: "One commits a mortal sin when there are simultaneously present: grave matter, full knowledge, and deliberate consent" *(Compendium of the Catechism,* 395).

Some common sins that constitute grave matter, according to the 2006 U.S. bishops' document, "Happy Are Those Who Are Called to His Supper":

Missing Mass – "Failing to worship God by missing Mass on Sundays and holy days of obligation without a serious reason, such as sickness or the absence of a priest"

Abortion and euthanasia – "Committing murder, including abortion and euthanasia, harboring deliberate hatred of others"

Any extramarital sexual activity – "Engaging in sexual activity outside the bonds of a valid marriage"

Theft – Including "serious fraud, or other immoral business practices"

Pornography – "Producing, marketing, or indulging in pornoraphy"

Slander, hatred, and envy – "Speaking maliciously or slandering people in a way that seriously undermines their good name. … Harboring deliberate hatred of others. … Engaging in envy that leads one to wish grave harm to someone else"

5. CONFESSION HELPS KEEP OUR SOULS TIDY.

Even if you aren't conscious of a serious sin, it is still highly recommended that you to go to confession regularly say, once a month. As Pope Benedict XVI put it: "It is very helpful to confess with a certain regularity. It is true: our sins are always the same, but we clean our homes, our rooms, at least once a week, even if the dirt is always the same; in order to live in cleanliness, in order to start again. Otherwise, the dirt might not be seen but it builds up. Something similar can be said about the soul" (Pope Benedict's meeting with children, St Peter's Square, October 15, 2005).

Confession Definition: "One commits a venial sin when, in a less serious matter, he does not observe the standard prescribed by the moral law, or when he disobeys the moral law in a grave matter, but without full knowledge or without complete consent" (CCC, 1862). ✣

10 THINGS YOU CAN EXPECT FROM CONFESSION

God doesn't make promises that he won't keep. Catholic teaching assures us a number of benefits that will come to us from confession. Here are ten from the Catechism of the Catholic Church.

1. PARDON AND MERCY

"Those who approach the sacrament of penance obtain pardon from God's mercy for the offense committed against him" (CCC, 1422).

2. RECONCILIATION

The sacrament reconciles us with the Church, with God, and can help reconcile us to those we have hurt (CCC, 1424).

3. A WELCOME FROM THE FATHER

Comparing our journey to the story of the prodigal son, the Catechism calls confession the "sacrament of conversion" and says it is "the first step in returning to the Father" (CCC, 1423).

4. A SECOND "BAPTISM"

We are first "converted" and become Christians at our baptism, but a second "conversion" is needed as we journey through our lives, says the Catechism (CCC, 1428). "St. Ambrose says of the two conversions that, in the Church, 'there are water and tears: the water of baptism and the tears of repentance'" (CCC, 1429).

5. INTERIOR CHANGE

Interior peace comes from interior repentance and penance, "a radical reorientation of our whole life, a return, a conversion to God with all our heart, an end of sin, a turning away from evil" (CCC, 1431).

6. A NEW HEART

"The human heart is heavy and hardened," says the Catechism. "God must give man a new heart. … It is in discovering the greatness of God's love that our heart is shaken by the horror and weight of sin" (CCC, 1432).

7. CONSOLATION

The world tells us that sin owns us, and that we can never change. The Holy Spirit has "proved the world wrong about sin" says the Catechism. The Holy Spirit is "the Consoler who gives the human heart grace for repentance and conversion" (CCC, 1433).

8. A JUST PENANCE

The penance that a priest gives "must correspond as far as possible with the gravity and nature of the sins committed. It can consist of prayer, an offering, works of mercy, service of neighbor, voluntary self-denial, sacrifices, and above all the patient acceptance of the cross we must bear" (CCC, 1460).

9. THE STRICTEST SECRECY

"Given the delicacy and greatness of this ministry and the respect due to persons, the Church declares that every priest who hears confessions is bound under very severe penalties to keep absolute secrecy regarding the sins that his penitents have confessed to him. He can make no use of knowledge that confession gives him about penitents' lives. This secret, which admits of no exceptions, is called the 'sacramental seal,' because what the penitent has made known to the priest remains 'sealed' by the sacrament" (CCC, 1467). "The sacramental seal is inviolable; therefore, it is a crime for a confessor in any way to betray a penitent by word or in any other manner or for any reason" (CCC, 2490; Canon 983).

10. STRENGTH FOR THE BATTLE

One of the effects of confession is "spiritual strength for the Christian battle" (CCC, 1496). After confession, it's easier to face the temptations that once defeated you and remain true to the path you were meant to walk with God. "The sacrament of Penance offers a new possibility to convert and to recover the grace of justification," says the Catechism (CCC, 1446). It even notes that the Fathers of the Church present this sacrament as a rescue boat "after the shipwreck which is the loss of grace." ✣

7 THINGS EXPECTED FROM YOU IN CONFESSION

A confessor can count on the Church to fulfill its promises. But the sacrament is not magic. It requires an investment on the part of the person confessing.

1. CONTRITION

The Catechism calls contrition "sorrow of the soul and detestation for the sin committed, together with the resolution not to sin again" (CCC, 1451). You have to have either perfect contrition or imperfect contrition. *Perfect contrition* "arises from a love by which God is loved above all else." *Imperfect contrition* is "born of the consideration of sin's ugliness or the fear of eternal damnation." Bottom line: You have to have contrition for your sins – ideally out of love for God, minimally from fear of God's judgment (CCC, 1452-1453).

2. EXAMINATION OF CONSCIENCE

The Catechism says that the sacrament "ought to be prepared for by an *examination of conscience* made in the light of the Word of God" (CCC, 1454). We offer some examples in this book.

3. DISCLOSURE OF SINS

The Catechism tells us that through the confession of sins a penitent "looks squarely at the sins he is guilty of, takes responsibility for them, and thereby opens himself again to God and to the communion of the Church in order to make a new future possible" (CCC, 1455).

4. CONFESSION TO A PRIEST

"...All mortal sins of which penitents after a diligent self-examination are conscious must be recounted by them in confession..." (CCC, 1456).

5. CONFESSION AT LEAST ONCE A YEAR

"'After having attained the age of discretion each of the faithful is bound by an obligation faithfully to confess serious sins at least once a year.' Anyone who is aware of having committed a mortal sin must not receive Holy Communion, even if he experiences deep contrition, without having first received sacramental absolution, unless he has a grave reason for receiving Communion and there is no possibility of going to confession. Children must go to the sacrament of Penance before receiving Holy Communion for the first time" (CCC, 1457).

6. SATISFACTION

"One must do what is possible in order to repair the harm of sins [e.g., return stolen goods, restore the reputation of someone slandered, pay compensation for injuries]...." (CCC, 1459).

7. PENANCE

"...Absolution takes away sin, but it does not remedy all the disorders sin has caused. Raised up from sin, the sinner must still recover his full spiritual health by doing something more to make amends for the sin..." (CCC, 1459).

7 OBJECTIONS AND THE BIBLE'S ANSWERS

Many of the common concerns we have about confession are answered in Scripture. Here are a few.

1. I don't really sin.

St. John says in his first letter that no one is immune: "If we say, 'We are without sin,' we deceive ourselves, and the truth is not in us" (1 Jn 1:8). And the Lord himself taught us to pray: "Forgive us our trespasses."

2. I don't need to go through a priest. I can confess my sins directly to God.

Not according to the Bible. In St. John's account of the Resurrection, we learn that Christ instituted the priesthood so that its members could be the ministers of his forgiveness: "On the evening of that first day of the week, when the doors were locked, where the disciples were, for fear of the Jews, Jesus came and stood in their midst and said to them, 'Peace be with you. …. As the Father has sent me, so I send you.' And when he had said this, he breathed on them and said to them, 'Receive the holy Spirit. Whose sins you forgive are forgiven them, and whose sins you retain are retained'" (Jn 20:19, 21-23). We do go to God for forgiveness, but we do it the way Jesus told us to.

3. God is someone we have a personal relationship with; no priest or other mediator should come between us.

It's true that we have a personal relationship with God, but he has always used human agents to facilitate that relationship, particularly with regards to sin. In the Old Testament we read that if any person "commits a sin and has guilt to bear…the priest shall then make atonement for his sin" (Lv 5:1,6). And also: "…the priest shall make atonement before the Lord for the sin he has committed, and it will be forgiven him" (Lv 19:22). Today, priests still perform what St. Paul calls the "ministry of reconciliation" (cf. 2 Cor 5:18). However, as soon as we realize that we have sinned, we should make a "perfect act of contrition" with the intention of going to confession as soon as possible.

4. Where is confession mentioned in the Bible?

In Numbers 5:7 we see the practice of publicly confessing sins and making restitution. Nehemiah 9:2-3 describes a confession ritual. Baruch 1:14 refers to the same kind of ritual. Sirach 4:26 gives good advice about confession: "Be not ashamed to acknowledge your guilt, but of your ignorance rather be ashamed."

The practice was common in the New Testament times as well. "People of the whole Judean countryside and all the inhabitants of Jerusalem were going out to [John the Baptist] and were being baptized by him in the Jordan River as they acknowledged their sins" (Mk 1:5; cf. Mt 3:5-6).

Often when people encountered Jesus they confessed their sins. Think of the woman at the well (Jn 4:17); Peter is inspired to confess by Christ's miracles (Lk 5:8); the woman with the hemorrhage tells "him the whole truth" and is given a cure (Mk 5:33).

The practice continued in the early Church. When the apostles told people the good news, these people were inspired to confess. "Many of those who had become believers came forward and openly acknowledged their former practices" (Acts 19:18). St. John explains that the New Testament practice of confession is transformational. "If we acknowledge our sins, he is faithful and just and will forgive our sins and cleanse us from every wrongdoing" (1 Jn 1:9).

5. I've had run-ins with priests in the past. those experiences have soured me on the idea that a priest's action is all that important.

St. Paul acknowledged that some people might have that kind of concern, even with someone like him, who was a saint. So he said, "What I have forgiven, if I have forgiven anything, has been for you in the presence of Christ" (2 Cor 2:10) or *in persona Christi,* which means "in the person of Christ" – in other words, acting with Christ or on his behalf. This is an ancient phrase, used regularly by Pope John Paul II.

Priests are only human. A penitent may have felt belittled, or may have felt ignored, or may have felt embarrassed because of something a priest said. But this isn't the usual way confession goes, and the priest is usually the first to admit that he is an imperfect vessel of this great power. Brush yourself off and try again.

6. I'm older (or wiser, or more advanced) than the priest, and it would feel funny confessing to him.

Remember: You're confessing to Christ, not the priest. And don't be surprised when you find a simple and personal message that touches you personally in the priest's humble words.

7. It just seems that the Catholic Church has complicated everything. For instance, the Bible never talks about "mortal" vs. "venial" sins. That doesn't sound like the kind of thing Jesus would say.

But Jesus said exactly this. Remember, he compared our lives to a servant in charge of a house. He said the master will come back when we least expect it to see how well his servant is taking care of the house. We'll be punished according to the severity of our sin, depending on whether or not we recognized our sinfulness: "That servant who knew his master's will but did not make preparations nor act in accord with his will shall be beaten severely; and the servant who was ignorant of his master's will but acted in a way deserving of a severe beating shall be beaten only lightly. Much will be required of the person entrusted with much, and still more will be demanded of the person entrusted with more" (Lk 12:47-48).

In the Sermon on the Mount, Jesus talks about deadly sins with great emphasis. We must confess and rid ourselves of mortal sins right away: "If your right eye causes you to sin, tear it out and throw it away. It is better for you to lose one of your members than to have your whole body thrown into Gehenna" (Mt 5:29).

But he also acknowledges that there are lesser sins that don't exclude you from the kingdom. They don't send you to "Gehenna," but they do impact you. "Therefore, whoever breaks one of the least of these commandments and teaches others to do so will be called least in the kingdom of heaven" (Mt 5:19).

St. John expounded on this distinction. It is from him that we get the name mortal (or death-causing) sin. "If anyone sees his brother sinning, if the sin is not deadly, he should pray to God and he will give him life. This is only for those whose sin is not deadly. There is such a thing as deadly sin, about which I do not say that you should pray. All wrongdoing is sin, but there is sin that is not deadly" (1 Jn 5:16-17). ✣

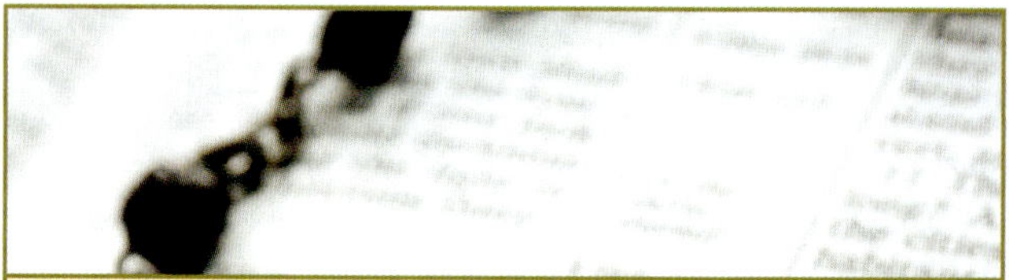

CATHOLICISM 101

Here are some basic formulas of the Catholic faith that are good to know as we go on to discuss confession and examine our consciences. A book could be written about any one of these, but sometimes it's helpful to have the bare facts laid out.

A CATHOLIC'S MOTTO

"I am third."

First = God. Second = others. Third = me.

THE GOSPEL ON 5 FINGERS

From Mother Teresa

Hold up one hand and count one word per finger: "I did it to him."

THE 2 COMMANDMENTS OF LOVE

From the Compendium of the Catechism

1. You shall love the Lord your God with all your heart, with all your soul, and with all your mind.
2. You shall love your neighbor as yourself.

THE GOLDEN RULE

Do to others as you would have them do to you.

THE 10 COMMANDMENTS

1. I am the Lord your God: you shall not have strange gods before me.
2. You shall not take the name of the Lord your God in vain.
3. Remember to keep holy the Lord's Day.
4. Honor your father and your mother.
5. You shall not kill.
6. You shall not commit adultery.
7. You shall not steal.
8. You shall not bear false witness against your neighbor.
9. You shall not covet your neighbor's wife.
10. You shall not covet your neighbor's goods.

FROM THE CATECHISM (PART THREE, SECTION TWO)

THE BEATITUDES

From the Compendium of the Catechism

Blessed are the poor in spirit, for theirs is the kingdom of heaven.
Blessed are they who mourn, for they will be comforted.
Blessed are the meek, for they will inherit the earth.
Blessed are they who hunger and thirst for righteousness, for they will be satisfied.
Blessed are the merciful, for they will be shown mercy.
Blessed are the pure of heart, for they will see God.
Blessed are the peacemakers, for they will be called children of God.
Blessed are those who are persecuted for righteousness' sake, for theirs is the kingdom of heaven.
Blessed are you when people revile you and persecute you and utter all kinds of evil against you falsely on my account.
Rejoice and be glad, for your reward will be great in heaven.

THE 3 THEOLOGICAL VIRTUES

1. Faith
2. Hope
3. Charity

THE 4 CARDINAL VIRTUES

1. Prudence
2. Justice
3. Fortitude
4. Temperance

THE 7 GIFTS OF THE HOLY SPIRIT

1. Wisdom
2. Understanding
3. Counsel
4. Fortitude
5. Knowledge
6. Piety
7. Fear of the Lord

THE 12 FRUITS OF THE HOLY SPIRIT

1. Charity
2. Joy
3. Peace
4. Patience
5. Kindness
6. Goodness
7. Generosity
8. Gentleness
9. Faithfulness
10. Modesty
11. Self-control
12. Chastity

THE 5 PRECEPTS OF THE CHURCH

From the Compendium of the Catechism

1. You shall attend Mass on Sundays and on holy days of obligation and remain free from work or activity that could impede

the sanctification of such days.
2. You shall confess your sins at least once a year.
3. You shall receive the sacrament of the Eucharist at least during the Easter season.
4. You shall observe the days of fasting and abstinence established by the Church.
5. You shall help to provide for the material needs of the Church.

THE 7 CORPORAL WORKS OF MERCY

1. Feed the hungry.
2. Give drink to the thirsty.
3. Clothe the naked.
4. Shelter the homeless.
5. Visit the sick.
6. Visit the imprisoned.
7. Bury the dead.

THE 7 SPIRITUAL WORKS OF MERCY

1. Counsel the doubtful.
2. Instruct the ignorant.
3. Admonish sinners.
4. Comfort the afflicted.
5. Forgive offenses.
6. Bear wrongs patiently.
7. Pray for the living and the dead.

THE 7 CAPITAL SINS

1. Pride
2. Covetousness
3. Lust
4. Anger
5. Gluttony
6. Envy
7. Sloth

THE 4 LAST THINGS

1. Death
2. Judgment
3. Hell
4. Heaven ✣

7 WAYS TO EXAMINE YOUR CONSCIENCE

"The reception of this sacrament ought to be prepared for by an examination of conscience made in the light of the Word of God. The passages best suited to this can be found in the Ten Commandments, the moral catechesis of the Gospels and the apostolic Letters, such as the Sermon on the Mount and the apostolic teachings" (CCC, 1454).

PROPERLY FORMED CONSCIENCE

"Conscience must be informed and moral judgment enlightened. A well-formed conscience is upright and truthful. It formulates its judgments according to reason, in conformity with the true good willed by the wisdom of the Creator. The education of conscience is indispensable for human beings who are subjected to negative influences and tempted by sin to prefer their own judgment and to reject authoritative teachings" (CCC, 1783).

"The education of the conscience is a lifelong task. From the earliest years, it awakens the child to the knowledge and practice of the interior law recognized by conscience. Prudent education teaches virtue; it prevents or cures fear, selfishness and pride, resentment arising from guilt, and feelings of complacency, born of human weakness and faults. The education of the conscience guarantees freedom and engenders peace of heart" (CCC, 1784).

"In the formation of conscience the Word of God is the light for our path; we must assimilate it in faith and prayer and put it into practice. We must also examine our conscience before the Lord's Cross. We are assisted by the gifts of the Holy Spirit, aided by the witness or advice of others and guided by the authoritative teaching of the Church" (CCC, 1785). ... "Conscience can remain in ignorance or make erroneous judgments. Such ignorance and errors are not always free of guilt" (CCC, 1801).

PRAYER TO THE HOLY SPIRIT AND INTERCESSION OF MARY, MOTHER OF MERCY

It's valuable to pray to the Holy Spirit for enlightenment and sincerity before an examination of conscience and to ask the intercession of Mary so that you might make a good confession.

Come Holy Spirit into my soul,
Enlighten my mind that I may know
the sins I ought to confess,
and grant me your grace to confess them fully,
humbly and with contrite heart.
Help me to firmly resolve not to commit them again.
Amen.

O Blessed Virgin,
Mother of my Redeemer,
mirror of innocence and sanctity,
and refuge of penitent sinners,
intercede for me through the Passion of Your Son,
that I may obtain the grace to make a good
confession. Amen.

אנכי ה
לא יהיה
לא תשא
זכור את
כבד את
לא תרצח
לא תנאף
לא תגנב
לא תענה
לא תחמד

1. THE TEN COMMANDMENTS

1. I am the Lord your God. You shall not have strange gods before me.

- Do I give God time every day in prayer?
- Do I seek to love him with my whole heart?
- Have I been involved with superstitious practices, or have I been involved with the occult?
- Do I seek to surrender myself to God's word as taught by the Church?
- Have I ever received Communion in the state of mortal sin?
- Have I ever deliberately told a lie in confession, or have I withheld a mortal sin from the priest in confession?
- Are there other "gods" in my life (money, security, power, people, etc.)?

2. You shall not take the name of the Lord your God in vain.

- Have I used God's name in vain: lightly or carelessly?
- Have I been angry with God?
- Have I wished evil upon any other person?
- Have I insulted a sacred person or abused a sacred object?

3. Remember to keep holy the Lord's Day.

- Have I deliberately missed Mass on Sundays or holy days of obligation?
- Have I tried to observe Sunday as a family day and a day of rest?
- Do I do needless work on Sunday?
- Do I shop unnecessarily on Sunday?
- Do I dress properly and act reverently in Church?

4. Honor your father and your mother.

- Do I honor and obey my parents?
- Have I neglected my duties to my spouse and children?
- Have I given my family a good religious example?
- Do I try to bring peace into my home life?
- Do I care for my aged and infirm relatives?

5. *You shall not kill.*
    - Have I had an abortion, or have I encouraged or helped anyone to have an abortion?
    - Have I physically harmed anyone?
    - Have I abused alcohol or drugs?
    - Did I give scandal to anyone, thereby leading him or her into sin?
    - Have I been angry or resentful?
    - Have I harbored hatred in my heart?
    - Have I mutilated myself through any form of sterilization?
    - Have I encouraged or condoned sterilization?
    - Have I engaged, in any way, in sins against human life, such as artificial insemination or in vitro fertilization?
    - Have I participated in or approved of euthanasia?
6. *You shall not commit adultery.*
    - Have I been faithful to my marriage vows in thought and action?
    - Have I engaged in any sexual activity outside of marriage?
    - Have I used any method of contraception or artificial birth control in my marriage?
    - Has each sexual act in my marriage been open to the transmission of new life?
    - Have I been guilty of masturbation?
    - Do I seek to control my thoughts and my imagination?
    - Have I respected all members of the opposite sex, or have I thought of other people as mere objects?
    - Have I been guilty of any homosexual activity?
    - Have I indulged in pornography?
    - Have I watched immoral programs on television or the Internet, or have I gone to immoral movies?
    - Do I seek to be chaste in my thoughts, words, and actions?
    - Am I careful to dress modestly?

7. *You shall not steal.*
   - Have I stolen what is not mine?
   - Have I returned or made restitution for what I have stolen?
   - Do I waste time at work, school, and home?
   - Do I gamble excessively, thereby depriving my family of their needs?
   - Do I pay my debts promptly?
   - Do I seek to share what I have with the poor?
   - Have I cheated anyone out of what is justly theirs – for example, creditors, insurance companies, or big corporations?
8. *You shall not bear false witness against your neighbor.*
   - Have I lied? Have I gossiped?
   - Do I speak badly of others behind their backs?
   - Am I sincere in my dealings with others?
   - Am I critical, negative, or uncharitable in my thoughts of others?
   - Do I keep secret what should be kept confidential?
   - Have I injured the reputation of others by slander?

9. *You shall not desire your neighbor's wife.*
   - Have I consented to impure thoughts?
   - Have I caused them by impure reading, movies, television, conversation, or curiosity?
   - Do I pray at once to banish impure thoughts and temptations?
   - Have I behaved in an inappropriate way with members of the opposite sex?

10. *You shall not desire your neighbor's goods.*
    - Am I jealous of what other people have?
    - Do I envy the families or possessions of others?
    - Am I greedy or selfish?
    - Are material possessions the center of my life?

2. LOOK AT YOUR LIFE

The Church recommends using the Sermon on the Mount to examine your conscience. You can find it in Matthew 5. Jesus set out the beatitudes, and calls Christians to a high level of moral living. Also, use the Catholic formulations from the previous chapter (beginning on p.34).

3. LOOK AT YOUR LOVE

The whole thirteenth chapter of 1 Corinthians is brief and excellent to read while reflecting on one's life. Especially read verses 4-7. Think of each word and ask yourself honestly, "Have I failed to love in this way?"

"Love is patient, love is kind. It is not jealous, [love] is not pompous, it is not inflated, it is not rude, it does not seek its own interests, it is not quick-tempered, it does not brood over injury, it does not rejoice over wrongdoing but rejoices with the truth. It bears all things, believes all things, hopes all things, endures all things."

4. LOOK AT YOUR WORDS

St. James sees charity in speech as a key to the moral life.

"If anyone does not fall short in speech, he is a perfect man, able to bridle his whole body also. If we put bits into the mouths of horses to make them obey us, we also guide their whole bodies. It is the same with ships: Even though they are so large and driven by fierce winds, they are steered by a very small rudder wherever the pilot's inclination wishes. In the same way the tongue is a small member and yet has great pretensions.

"Consider how small a fire can set a huge forest ablaze. The tongue is also a fire. It exists among our members as a world of malice, defiling the whole body and setting the entire course of our lives on fire, itself set on fire by Gehenna. For every kind of beast and bird, of reptile and sea creature, can be tamed and has been tamed by the human species, but no human being can tame the tongue. It is a restless evil, full of deadly poison. With it we bless the Lord and Father, and with it we curse human beings who are made in the likeness of God. From the same mouth come blessing and cursing. This need not be so, my brothers. Does a spring gush forth from the same opening both pure and brackish water? Can a fig tree, my brothers, produce olives, or a grapevine figs? Neither can salt water yield fresh" (Jas 3:2-12).

5. A NEW YOU

In his letter to the Colossians, St. Paul sums up what you have to leave behind if you are to be a new person in Christ:

"If then you were raised with Christ, seek what is above, where Christ is seated at the right hand of God. Think of what is above, not of what is on earth. For you have died, and your life is hidden with Christ in God. When Christ your life appears, then you too will appear with him in glory.

"Put to death, then, the parts of you that are earthly: immorality, impurity, passion, evil desire, and the greed that is idolatry. Because of these the wrath of God is coming [upon the disobedient]. By these you too once conducted yourselves, when you lived in that way.

"But now you must put them all away: anger, fury, malice, slander, and obscene language out of your mouths. Stop lying to one another, since you have taken off the old self with its practices and have put on the new self, which is being renewed, for knowledge, in the image of its creator" (Col 3:1-10).

6. LOOK AT YOUR RELATIONSHIPS

1. *My relationship with God*
   - Am I generous in the way I live the precepts of the Church?
   - Did I skip Sunday Mass? Did I skip it with my heart and/or my mind? Did I try to make the most of it, even if distracted? Did I tune it out and not try to tune back in?
   - Have I been "saying" my prayers instead of *praying* my prayers?
   - Do I send God away and block him out of certain areas of my life – social life, leisure life, work life, studies, etc.?

2. *My relationship with others*
   - Am I generous in the way I love my neighbor as myself?
   - Do I put myself at the service of others, or do I more or less use them?
   - Do I show my spouse love in words and actions? Do I respect my spouse enough to be honest?
   - How am I with my children? Am I careful about the example I set? Do I realize they're watching me?
   - How am I with my friends? Do I always make things go my way? Do I go along with them, even in what is morally offensive? Do I initiate or participate in gossip?
   - How am I with my employer? Do I make the best use of my time? Do I treat my employer with gratitude for employing me?
   - How about my parents and others in my family? Do I honor them all with the respect they deserve?

3. *My relationship with myself*
   - Do I battle the seven capital sins?
   - Am I another person when I am alone? Am I another person in my thoughts? Do I think things about others I would never say? Or do I strive to live the Golden Rule, even in my heart?
   - Do I live my Christian principles when no one is watching? Online? At work? In what I read? In what I watch? In what I listen to? In the car?
   - Every Sunday I confess to faults in what I have done and in what I have failed to do. What good have I failed to do? ✣

7. 20 QUESTIONS FOR YOUNG PEOPLE

1. Did I pay attention at Mass? Have I fooled around in Church?
2. Did I say my prayers every day?
3. Did I say mean things to my mom or dad?
4. Did I always say "Thank you" when I should have?
5. Am I hard to get along with (at school, at Grandma's, at home)?
6. Did I do what my mom and dad told me to do? My teacher?
7. Was I lazy around the house? Did I do my chores?
8. Did I hurt others people's feelings by calling them bad names?
9. Have I started fights with my brothers and sisters at home?
10. Have I blamed other people for things I do? Did I get other people into trouble?
11. Do I hit people when I get mad?
12. Have I forgiven people, or am I holding a grudge?
13. Have I cheated or been unfair in games?
14. Did I refuse to play with someone for no good reason?
15. Was I was lazy about my schoolwork?
16. Did I fail to do my homework?
17. Did I cheat in school?
18. Did I ever lie to my parents? My teachers? My friends?
19. Did I take anything that didn't belong to me?
20. Did I avoid medicine? Did I refuse to eat food I didn't like?

THE 6-STEP HOW-TO GUIDE TO CONFESSION

Individual confession and absolution *is the only ordinary way for the faithful to reconcile themselves with God and the church, unless physical or moral impossibility prevents this.* **Communal penance** services *allow the examination of conscience to take place in a group setting, but individual confession is necessary for absolution except in rare extreme emergencies, as Pope John Paul II stressed in his 2002* Motu Proprio *document* Misericordia Dei. *"Grave necessity of this sort can arise when there is imminent danger of death without sufficient time for the priest or priests to hear each penitent's confession. Grave necessity can also exist when, given the number of penitents, there are not enough confessors to hear individual confessions properly in a reasonable time, so that the penitents through no fault of their own would be deprived of sacramental grace or Holy Communion for a long time. In this case, for the absolution to be valid the faithful must have the intention of individually confessing their grave sins in the time required. The diocesan bishop is the judge of whether or not the conditions required for* **general absolution** *exist. A large gathering of the faithful on the occasion of major feasts or pilgrimages does not constitute a case of grave necessity."* (CCC, 1483; Canon 961, 962).

HOW TO GO TO CONFESSION

1. You always have the option to go to confession anonymously, that is, behind a screen. You may have the option of going to confession face-to-face as well – but only if the priest offers it. He can insist on your anonymity if he wishes.

2. After the priest greets you in the name of Christ, make the sign of the cross. He may choose to recite a reading from Scripture, after which you say: "Bless me, Father, for I have sinned. It has been (state how long) since my last confession. These are my sins."

3. Tell your sins simply and honestly to the priest. You might even want to discuss the circumstances and the root causes of your sins and ask the priest for advice or direction. However, avoid explanations that are really excuses or rationalizations for your sin. You are here to own up to what you have done. The best confessions are simple, honest, and to the point.

4. Listen to the advice the priest gives you and accept the penance from him. Then make an act of contrition for your sins.

ACT OF CONTRITION

From the Compendium of the Catechism of the Catholic Church

O my God, I am heartily sorry for having offended thee, and I detest all my sins because of thy just punishments, but most of all because they offend thee, my God, who art all good and deserving of all my love. I firmly resolve with the help of thy grace to sin no more and to avoid the near occasion of sin. Amen.

5. The priest will then absolve you, using these words: "God, the Father of mercies, through the death and resurrection of his Son has reconciled the world to himself and sent the Holy Spirit among us for the forgiveness of sins; through the ministry of the Church may God give you pardon and peace, and I absolve you from your sins in the name of the Father, and of the Son, and of the Holy Spirit. Amen." Then he will dismiss you. Sometimes he will use the words of praise: "Give thanks to the Lord for he is good." You may respond: "For his mercy endures forever." The priest will then conclude with: "The Lord has freed you from your sins. Go in peace." You may respond by saying: "Thanks be to God."

6. Spend some time with Our Lord thanking and praising him for the gift of his mercy. Perform your penance as soon as possible – in the church, if you can. ✣

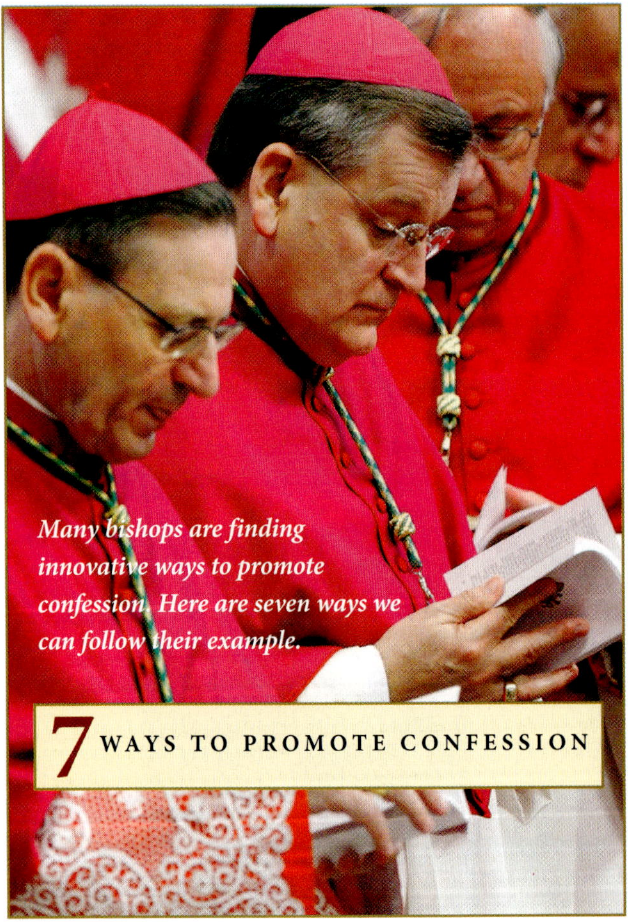

7 WAYS TO PROMOTE CONFESSION

Many bishops are finding innovative ways to promote confession. Here are seven ways we can follow their example.

1. GO REGULARLY YOURELF

Our example evangelizes more than we know, and others will notice the witness in our lives. And sometimes priests can be tempted to give up waiting in a confessional for penitents who never come. If you give them some business, you will help ensure that they'll continue to make themselves available.

Quick tip: *A friendly "Thanks for being here for us, Father," doesn't hurt, either.*

2. BRING YOUR FAMILY – ESPECIALLY CHILDREN AND THE ELDERLY WHO CAN'T GET OUT

Don't forget that children need to go to confession. Some writers have stressed the negative aspects of childhood confession – being lined up in their Catholic schools and "forced to think of things to feel guilty about." It needn't be like that. Confession can give children a place to unburden themselves without fear, a place to get kindly adult advice when they are worried about speaking to their parents. Many families make confession an outing, followed by ice cream or coffee.

Quick tip: *An examination of conscience for children is available at NCRegister.com – click "Resources" then "Confessional Guides."*

3. MENTION IT TO OTHERS

We often think of confession as unmentionable. But there's no reason not to tell people that we've gone to confession. If we don't, aren't we tacitly suggesting that there is something shameful and dark about this joyful, healthy sacrament? Why not share with others the peace and joy we've received in confession?

Quick tip: *Since confession is a significant event in our lives, it's an appropriate answer to the question, "What did you do last weekend?"*

4. LEARN, THEN SPREAD YOUR KNOWLEDGE

There are many books and pamphlets on confession (see the Resources section at the end of this booklet). Consider placing materials on confession on your parish's pamphlet rack, with your pastor's permission. Have some material on hand to give to others as the opportunity arises.

Quick tip: *The* National Catholic Register's *own reader-friendly "How and Why to Go to Confession" is available for free at NCRegister.com. Click on Resources, and then on the "How to Be a Catholic Guides."*

5. FOLLOW THE POPE

Pope Benedict XVI is an eloquent spokesperson for confession. "Jesus Christ is divine mercy in person: Encountering Christ means encountering the mercy of God," he said in his homily before the conclave that elected him. "The mercy of Christ is not a cheap grace; it does not presume a trivialization of evil. Christ carries in his body and on his soul all the weight of evil, and all its destructive force. He burns and transforms evil through suffering, in the fire of his suffering love."

Quick tip: *Following Pope John Paul II, Pope Benedict XVI recommends the Divine Mercy devotion, which places a special emphasis on confession.*

6. CHILDREN: USE YOUR POWER

Parents should lead the way to virtuous living – as one priest put it, the failure to take children to Sunday Mass and confession is spiritual child abuse. Many parents rediscover confession through their children.

When a girl asked Pope Benedict if she could take the initiative in leading her parents back to the sacraments, he told her: "I would think so – of course, with great love and great respect for your parents, because they certainly have a lot to do. However, with a daughter's respect and love, you could say to them: 'Dear Mommy, dear Daddy, it is so important for us all, even for you, to meet Jesus. This encounter enriches us. It is an important element in our lives. Let's find a little time together; we can find an opportunity. Perhaps there is also a possibility where Grandma lives.'"

Quick tip: *Kids have led their families into all sorts of healthy practices, from recycling to quitting smoking. Why not confession?*

7. MENTION IT AS A KIND OF "EXCUSE"

If someone invited you on a walk through the mud, you'd say, "No thanks, I don't want to have to clean my shoes and clothes." When someone begins to engage in denigrating gossip, or wants you to watch an objectionable movie, or suggests plans that make it impossible to go to Mass on Sunday, the same answer is available. "No thanks, I would to have to figure out how to get to confession again before my regularly scheduled time!"

Quick Tip: *The offhand comment, "I won't be able to make it until later, because I want to get to confession," can be more convicting than a theological discourse.* ✣

RESOURCES

Catechism of the Catholic Church (Sections 1420-1498)

The Rite of Penance (Ordo Paenitentiae), a Vatican document issued Dec 2, 1974

"Reconciliation and Penance," Pope John Paul II, Apostolic Exhortation, December 2, 1984

Circular Letter Concerning the Integrity of the Sacrament of Penance, Congregation for Divine Worship and the Discipline of the Sacraments, March 20, 2000

"Rediscovering the Sacrament of Reconciliation," Pope John Paul II, Holy Thursday Letter, March 25, 2001

Misericordia Dei, Apostolic Letter in the Form of *Motu Proprio* on Certain Aspects of the Celebration of the Sacrament of Penance, Pope John Paul II, April 7, 2002

"The Sins We Commit Distance Us from God," address of Pope Benedict XVI delivered before praying the midday Angelus on February 15, 2009, with those gathered in St. Peter's Square

Lord, Have Mercy: The Healing Power of Confession, Dr. Scott Hahn, Doubleday Religion, 2003

Personal Encounter with Jesus Christ: The Sacrament of Reconciliation, Copyright © Rosary Evangelization Apostolate Inc., 2010